TM

The Gadget Scientist Guide to Using Your Digital Camera

Mark Burton

85 / 250

The Gadget Scientist Guide to Using Your Digital Camera

Mark Burton

Published in the United Kingdom by The Gadget Scientist, an imprint of Burtonia Communications Ltd
5th Floor, 7-10 Chandos Street, London W1G 9DQ
www.burtoniacommunications.co.uk

© 2010 Burtonia Communications Ltd

First Edition

Contact **info@gadgetscientist.com** with questions or comments. Please do not send confidential or proprietary information.

Notice of Rights

Notice of Liability

Trademarks

British Library Cataloguing in Publication Data

A catalogue record for this book is available from the British Library.

ISBN 13: 978-0-9560321-0-2
ISBN 10: 0-9560321-0-9

Photography: Mark Burton   **Editor:** Bronwyn Goodwin
Illustrations: Anthony Rule   **Graphic design:** Nicky Taylor

Printed and bound in the United Kingdom by MWL Print Group.

10 9 8 7 6 5 4 3 2 1

Contents

Thank you to Bronwyn for her editing,
Anthony for his illustrations and
Nicky for her designs.

Thanks also to my friends and family
for being models, for their numerous suggestions
and for their enthusiasm!

Chapter 2 - Taking Photos

Chapter 3 - Advanced Settings

Chapter 4 - How Do I?

Chapter 5 - Technical Tips

Using this guide

You can read **The Gadget Scientist Guide to Using Your Digital Camera** from beginning to end, or just dip in and out when you have a particular question or problem.

GADGET TIP! Keep an eye out for the **Gadget Tips!** These include hints and tricks.

INVESTIGATE! Try out these activities to explore the features and functions on your digital camera.

Cross and Tick!

The Gadget Scientist Guide includes instructions on how to fix common photo problems.

Experiment!

The **Experiment!** page at the end of each chapter includes activities to try on your camera. Many of them can be done without leaving your favourite chair!

The Gadget Scientist cameras

The Gadget Scientist cameras

There are lots of different makes and models of digital cameras available. They come in all different shapes, sizes and even colours.

This book uses two example digital cameras to guide you through the common features and functions.

Delete and flash: these icons are found on most digital cameras

If your camera doesn't look exactly like the example cameras don't worry! Just look for the similarities between your camera and the Gadget Scientist cameras.

This guide concentrates on basic photography principles and the most widely used features and functions. So if you buy a new camera everything you've learnt will still apply.

Features of point-and-shoot digital cameras

Your camera might not look **exactly** like these illustrations, but this Gadget Scientist example camera is to help guide you to the same features on your camera.

1 Capture button (shutter release)
2 On/Off button
3 Microphone
4 Viewfinder
5 Mode selector
6 Flash
7 Lens
8 Battery and memory card slots
9 Digital input/output

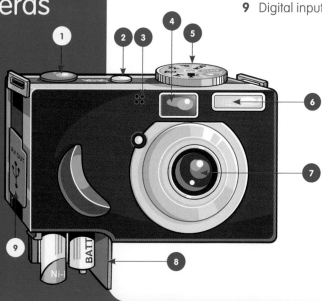

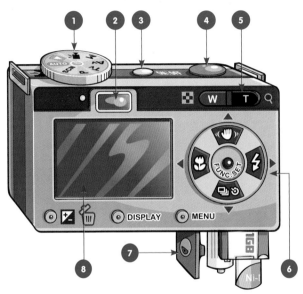

1 Mode selector
2 Viewfinder
3 On/Off button
4 Capture button (shutter release)
5 Wide-angle and telephoto (zoom)
6 Navigation buttons
7 Battery and memory card slots
8 Camera screen

INVESTIGATE! Which of these features are available on your digital camera?

Features of DSLR cameras

1 Capture button
  (shutter release)
2 Red-eye reduction
  and self-timer lamp
3 Flash
4 Flash pop-up button
5 Mode selector
6 Lens
7 Lens release
8 Digital input/output
9 Zoom ring
10 Focus ring

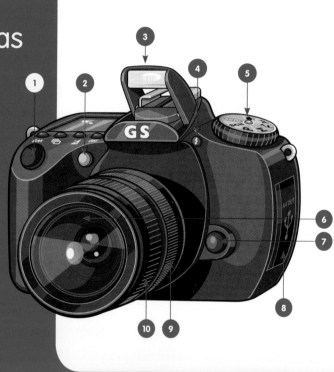

1 Mode selector
2 Viewfinder
3 Shutter speed dial
4 Top screen
5 Memory card slot
6 Battery slot
7 Aperture (f-number) dial
8 Camera screen
9 On/Off button

GADGET TIP! DSLR stands for Digital Single-Lens Reflex.

Digital camera modes

Most digital cameras have at least two modes: **AUTO** mode and **PLAY** mode. Others, like the Gadget Scientist cameras, have more!

Point-and-shoot: a basic selection of modes

DSLR or advanced point-and-shoot: basic and creative modes

The modes on the Gadget Scientist camera are used for:

 AUTO: taking photos

 PLAY: viewing and erasing photos and videos

 VIDEO: taking short videos

 SCENE: taking photos in specific situations e.g. at the beach or when watching fireworks

Creative modes: using the advanced settings and changing exposure values

Find out more about **creative modes** in **Chapter 3: Advanced Settings**

 **PLAY** mode

PLAY mode is for viewing captured photos or videos.

To scroll backwards and forwards through photos or videos use the navigation buttons adjacent to the camera screen.

Backwards   Forwards

🗑 ERASE button

To **erase** photos, use the button which looks like a dustbin or trash can. Only do this if you really want to get rid of a photo, as after it's erased you can't get it back!

Cancel   Erase   All

GADGET TIP! Make sure you erase only one photo at a time, and don't accidentally select the **ALL** option. This erases everything on your memory card.

SCN SCENE mode

In **SCENE** mode (sometimes called **BEST SHOT**), the camera adjusts all of the settings, based on the type of **SCENE** selected.

SCENE mode works best when you understand which of the settings the camera is changing.

For example, the **Fireworks SCENE** automatically selects a slow shutter speed to capture the colourful explosions so a tripod, or something stable, is necessary to prevent camera shake.

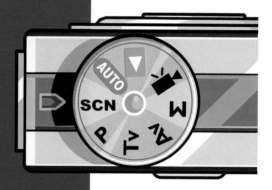

Find out more about **SCENE** mode in **Chapter 4: How do I?**

Portrait

Sports

Beach

Landscape

Kids & Pets

Fireworks

Snow

Night Scene

Night Snapshot

GADGET TIP! SCENE modes can be selected in the **MENU**, or on some cameras by using the mode selector dial.

 VIDEO mode

The **VIDEO** mode can be an unexpected bonus on digital cameras. However video recording times can be quite short, sometimes only 30 seconds, so don't start recording too early.

For the best sound quality try not to:

- cover the microphone with your fingers, as this muffles the sound, or
- record in windy conditions, as this distorts the sound.

Finger over microphone

Camera held correctly

GADGET TIP! Record video using the largest file size available. Videos recorded using a small file size can look blurry when viewed on a computer or television screen.

The MENU

The **MENU** is used to change settings. It is usually accessed by pushing the **MENU** button and is displayed on the camera screen.

The Gadget Scientist digital camera **MENU** has three tabs:

📷 **The CAMERA tab:** settings that apply when taking photos. For example, changing the focusing system, or turning red-eye reduction on or off.

The PLAY tab:
settings that apply when
viewing photos or videos.

The TOOLS tab:
basic camera options, for
example language, date/
time and the brightness of the
camera screen.

INVESTIGATE! Which **MENU** settings are displayed on your camera screen?

The camera screen

Many cameras display the current settings on the camera screen. The display is usually turned on and off by using the **Display** button.

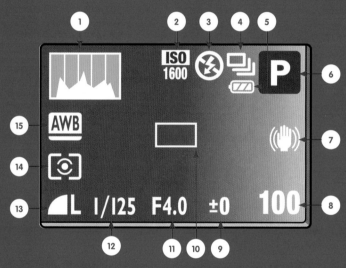

GADGET TIP! Your camera screen might not look exactly like the one above, but many of the icons will be similar.

camera basics

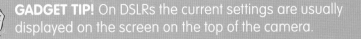

GADGET TIP! On DSLRs the current settings are usually displayed on the screen on the top of the camera.

Dual-purpose buttons

On some cameras there are buttons with two purposes.

They have one function when taking photos and a different one in **PLAY** mode. To identify them, look for buttons with two icons next to them.

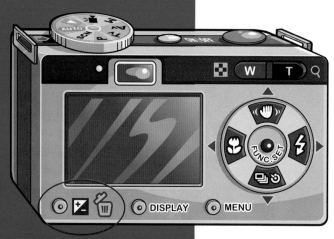

For example:

When taking photos this button selects the exposure compensation setting.

In **PLAY** mode this button is used to erase photos or videos.

INVESTIGATE! Does your camera have any dual-purpose buttons?

Experiment!

After you've read this chapter try the activities on the opposite page.

You can do these activities from the comfort of your favourite chair!

1. Find the **memory card** and **battery** slots and make sure you have a battery and memory card in your camera.

2. Turn your camera on and change between **camera modes.**

3. Which features, functions and icons does your camera share with the Gadget Scientist camera?

4. Change to **SCENE** mode (sometimes called **BEST SHOT**). Which **SCENE** modes does your camera support?

5. Change to **VIDEO** mode and take a short video.

6. Go to the camera **MENU** and scroll through the different options.

Find out more about memory cards and batteries in **Chapter 5: Technical Tips**

AUTO **AUTO** and the basic settings

When using **AUTO** the camera automatically sets the exposure values and advanced settings. For example **shutter speed, aperture, ISO** and **white balance.**

Depending on the make and model of camera, some basic settings can be selected and changed when using **AUTO.**

This chapter covers taking photos using the basic settings.

Single-shot, continuous and self-timer setting
(pages 36-39)

Zoom
(pages 40-43)

Focusing systems
(pages 48-57)

Close-up photos
(macro)
(pages 58-59)

Image stabilisation
(pages 64-65)

Flash and red-eye
reduction (pages 66-71)

GADGET TIP! On some cameras the basic settings may only be available in a **creative mode.**

Single-shot and continuous photos

Most digital cameras have an option to change between single-shot, continuous and self-timer settings.

Single-shot

Continuous or 'burst'

Self-timer (page 38)

Single-shot
When using **single-shot** the camera takes one photo at a time.

Continuous or 'burst'

In **continuous** the camera takes several photos in fast succession. This is great for photographing children in action.

GADGET TIP! After capturing several shots using the **continuous** setting, the camera will pause to record all of the photos, so be patient!

⏱ Self-timer

Don't miss out on the opportunity to be in the photo too!

When using **self-timer** the camera takes a photo after a short delay. On some cameras you can change the length of this delay, but 10 seconds is usually needed to get everyone ready.

GADGET TIP! Self-timer photos don't need a tripod. The camera can be rested on a wall or table. However, make sure it's a safe and stable surface and there is no danger of the camera falling on the ground.

Using zoom

To make subjects appear closer or further away in photos use **zoom.**

On point-and-shoot cameras zoom buttons are usually labelled **W** and **T**. They stand for **wide-angle** and **telephoto**. **W** zooms out, and **T** zooms in.

The zoom buttons can also be identified by a checkerboard and magnifying glass icon, or on some cameras by three small trees and one large tree.

Wide-angle

Telephoto

GADGET TIP! Zoom in and out on DSLR cameras by twisting the zoom ring on the lens.

Optical and digital zoom

Wide angle (no zoom)

Optical zoom

Optical zoom uses the camera lens to magnify the subject in a similar way to binoculars. This type of zoom captures a high quality photo.

Some cameras display the level of magnification on the camera screen using a zoom bar or magnification number (for example 6.0x).

Many cameras also have **digital zoom**. This isn't really zoom at all because the lens doesn't move! Instead, the camera digitally crops and enlarges part of the original image which produces a lower quality photo.

Some cameras indicate **digital zoom** by changing the colour of the zoom bar or magnification number.

Digital zoom

GADGET TIP! If you need to zoom when taking photos of people the easiest thing to do is to move closer to them!

How to focus

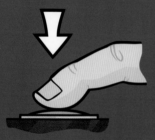

1. Push the capture button (shutter release) halfway down. The camera focuses on the subject in the focus point.

Focus point white: still trying to focus

2. When the camera has focused, the focus point changes colour and the camera may also beep. Push the capture button (shutter release) all the way down to take the photo.

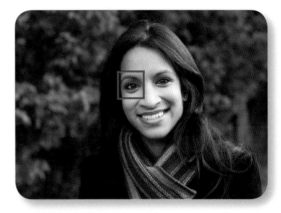

Focus point red: subject now in focus

GADGET TIP! The colours (and sound) of the focus point can differ between makes and models of cameras, but the concept of the focus point changing colour is the same.

Focus lock

To focus accurately use the **focus lock** technique.

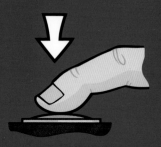

1. Aim the centre focus point at the subject.
2. Focus by pushing the capture button (shutter release) halfway down. This **locks** the focus.

3. Carefully recompose the shot, while still holding the capture button (shutter release) halfway down. Even though the focus point is no longer pointing at the subject, they will still be in focus.

4. Push the capture button (shutter release) all the way down to take the photo.

GADGET TIP! The **focus lock** technique should work with most focusing systems.

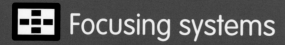 Focusing systems

The four primary focusing systems available on digital cameras are:

- **Centre**
- **Auto focus**
- **Face detection**
- **Flexible focus point**

The focusing system can be set in the **MENU**, or on some cameras by using a focus button. The focus points are shown in the viewfinder or on the camera screen.

Focusing system icon
Sometimes confused with the wide-angle icon (see page 41).

Single focus point

Digital cameras use one or more focus points to select and focus on subjects. For example, the **centre focus** system uses one focus point.

Multiple focus points

The combination and number of focus points can change. This depends on the focusing system selected and the number of subjects in the photo.

INVESTIGATE! Which focusing systems are available on your camera? How do you select them?

Centre focus system

Centre focus system: the camera focuses in the middle of the camera screen or viewfinder, and the focus point stays in the centre.

When **centre focus** is used with focus lock the photographer is in complete control of where the camera is focusing. This makes it the preferred choice of many professional photographers.

Watch out for:
the focus point
missing the subjects
and focusing on the
background instead.

GADGET TIP! For the best results when using the **centre focus** system use the **focus lock** technique.

Auto focus system

Auto focus system: the camera focuses on distinctive objects near the camera. In this example the focus points have correctly focused on the people.

Watch out for: the focus points selecting the wrong subject. In this example, it is the glass in the foreground.

GADGET TIP! If the camera selects the wrong subject, move, and recompose the photo until the camera focuses correctly.

Face detection system

Face detection system: the camera automatically focuses on faces. In this example the focus points have correctly focused on the two faces, and the camera confirms this.

2 faces detected

Watch out for:
the focus points selecting the wrong person.

The **face detection** system may not work if there is no one in the photo, so change to a different focusing system for landscapes.

1 face detected

GADGET TIP! If the camera focuses on the wrong person recompose the photo, or just wait until the other person has moved away.

Flexible focus point system

Flexible focus point:
one focus point can
be moved around
the camera screen
or viewfinder. In this
example the focus point
has been manually
moved to focus on the
subject near the edge of
the photo.

Watch out for:
the camera incorrectly focusing on the background, even though the focus point has been moved somewhere else.

GADGET TIP! On some cameras the **flexible focus point** system is not reliable. To select a specific subject use the **centre focus** system with the **focus lock** technique instead.

🌷 Macro focus

Point-and-shoot cameras usually have a minimum focusing distance of about 50 centimetres (20 inches), which means close-up photos taken with a standard setting will be out of focus.

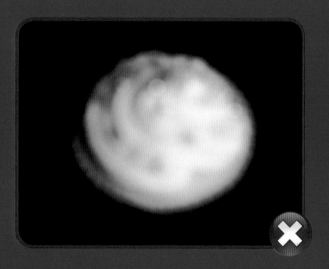

To take close-up photos, turn on the **macro** setting. The minimum focusing distance will now be about 15 centimetres (6 inches) and close-up photos will be in focus.

 To turn on **macro** push the 'flower' button.

GADGET TIP! Make sure **macro** is turned off when taking normal (and not close-up) photos.

Focus assist beam

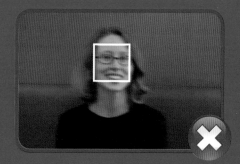

In low light conditions cameras may not be able to focus. This is because the focusing systems can't distinguish faces or high-contrast objects when it's too dark.

If this happens the focus points won't appear in the viewfinder or on the camera screen, or they will appear but won't change colour.

Some cameras have a **focus assist beam**. When it is turned on a camera can focus more effectively in low light conditions.

The bright focus assist beam can sometimes be annoying to subjects, so only use it when you really need to.

INVESTIGATE! Does your camera have a **focus assist beam?** If it does, this setting can usually be turned on and off in the **MENU.**

Common focus problems

There are some situations when cameras cannot focus.

Problem:
Strong light behind the subject

Solution:
Take the photo from a different angle

Problem:
Complicated patterns

Solution:
Take the photo from a different angle

Image stabilisation setting

A common cause of blurry photos is **camera shake.** This happens in low light conditions when the hand holding the camera moves during the extra time needed to capture a photo.

In these conditions, some camera screens show a flashing red camera icon, to warn that the photo will be blurry.

The **image stabilisation** or **anti-blur** feature, which is available on some digital cameras, reduces the effect of **camera shake.**

If the conditions are too dark for the **image stabilisation** or **anti-blur** feature to be effective, the flashing red camera icon will re-appear.

When this happens use a tripod, rest the camera on a stable surface, or use the flash.

Find out more about **low light photography** in **Chapter 4: How do I?**

taking photos

65

⚡ Flash settings

The standard flash setting provides additional light when taking photos in low light or dark conditions.

On point-and-shoot cameras there are settings
to turn the flash on and off, select the red-eye
reduction setting or use Auto flash.

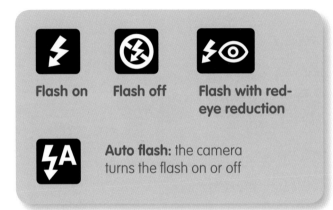

Flash on   **Flash off**   **Flash with red-eye reduction**

Auto flash: the camera turns the flash on or off

GADGET TIP! Some cameras have a flash that 'pops-up'. In **AUTO** the flash usually pops-up automatically. In **creative modes** use the flash pop-up button.

Using flash

Too far away
Flash photos can be too bright or too dark when subjects are too near or too far away.

Too near
In these situations the camera doesn't select the correct amount of flash to use.

For the best results take flash photos about 2 metres (6 feet) away from your subjects.

If your flash photos are still too bright or too dark use the **exposure compensation** setting (see page 120).

⚡👁 Red-eye reduction

A common problem with flash photography is that people's eyes look red. This occurs when light from the camera's flash reflects from the retina of the eye.

The **red-eye reduction** setting helps prevent red-eye. It sends a small blink of light before the photo is taken, which helps contract the iris and reduces reflection.

GADGET TIP! Red-eye reduction is great for portraits, but not action shots. The delay between pressing the capture button and the photo being taken means you might miss something!

Tripods

There are lots of different types of tripods available. Pocket-sized tripods are ideal if you are going on holiday and don't want to travel with anything larger.

Flexible tripods work just like normal tripods. They can also cling to branches, chairs or other objects.

A wall, or stack of books can be excellent improvised tripods, but make sure they are stable and there is no risk of your camera falling on the ground.

Experiment!

After you've read this chapter try the activities on the opposite page.

You can do these activities from the comfort of your favourite chair!

1. Set the camera to **AUTO** and take a photo using the **single-shot** setting.

2. Set the camera to **continuous** and take a burst of photos.

3. Use the **self-timer** setting and take a photo of yourself!

4. Take a photo using **wide-angle** and one using **telephoto** (zoom).

5. Identify the **focusing systems** on your camera.

6. Experiment with each **focusing system.** You can do this by taking photos of nearby objects or people.

7. Take a close-up photo using **macro.**

8. Take a photo using **flash.**

9. Turn the flash off, and take a photo using **image stabilisation.**

10. Take two flash photos of someone. One with **red-eye reduction,** and one without.

Beyond **AUTO**

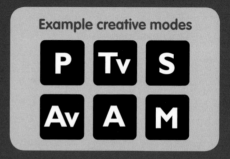

Example creative modes

In **AUTO** the camera automatically selects the exposure values and advanced settings.

This makes **AUTO** great for beginners, but frustrating if the settings are incorrect as adjustments can't be made.

To set the exposure values manually use a **creative mode.**

The **creative modes** give more control over the exposure values of **shutter speed, aperture (f-number)** and **ISO.**

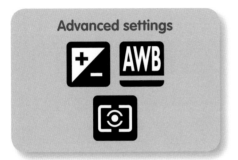

Advanced settings

When using **creative modes** the advanced settings can also be adjusted.

These include **exposure compensation, white balance** and the **light meter** settings.

This chapter covers:

- **exposure values**
- how and when to use the **creative modes** and
- how and when to use the **advanced settings.**

Exposure values

The correct combination of exposure values creates a photo that isn't too bright or too dark.

The exposure values are:

- **Shutter speed** or **Time value**: the amount of time the shutter is open
- **Aperture value** or **f-number:** the size of the lens opening that lets light into the camera
- **ISO**: the sensitivity of the camera's image sensor to light.

Balanced exposure

Underexposed

If too little light is let into the lens the photo becomes too dark or **underexposed**.

Overexposed

If too much light is let into the lens the photo becomes too bright or **overexposed**.

Calculating exposure values

When the capture button (shutter release) is pushed halfway down, a light reading is taken. The camera then calculates exposure values based on this reading.

 In **AUTO** the camera calculates all of the exposure values.

Example creative modes

When using a **creative mode** the camera calculates only some of the exposure values, and the user sets the others.

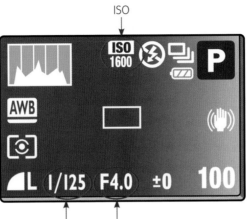

ISO

Shutter speed   Aperture / f-number

In a **creative mode** the exposure values and advanced setting details are usually shown on the camera screen, or on a small screen on the top of the camera. Many point-and-shoot cameras have an option to hide or show these photo settings.

INVESTIGATE! Set your camera to a **creative mode** and look for the exposure values on the camera screen.

Exposure values: **Shutter speed**

Shutter speed describes how quickly a photo is taken. It is measured in fractions of a second.

For example, if the shutter is open for one hundredth of a second, it is specified as '1/100'.

Shutter speeds between 1/125 and 1/250 are ideal for daytime portraits and landscape photography.

1/500

1/60

A **very fast shutter speed** freezes action and movement. Most sports photography uses fast shutter speeds.

Action photos need a fast shutter speed or the subject can look blurry. This is because the subject moves in between the shutter opening and closing.

Shutter speed examples

1/80: slow shutter speed

In dark conditions a slow shutter speed is necessary. This is because the shutter has to stay open longer to capture any available light.

1/40: very slow shutter speed

Photos taken with shutter speeds less than 1/80 can look blurry because the camera shakes in between the shutter opening and closing.

In very dark conditions the shutter speed necessary for a balanced exposure can be several seconds long.

The slow shutter speed, however, can result in camera shake and the photo can be blurry.

To take photos that aren't blurry use a tripod or rest the camera on a stable surface.

Exposure values: **Aperture**

The **aperture** value describes how wide or narrow the lens opening is.

Inside nearly every camera lens is a small diaphragm. It can be opened or closed to let in more or less light.

The size of the opening is called the **aperture** and is measured with an **f-number.** For example, f/4.0 or f/5.6.

f/8.0: narrow aperture

Only a small amount of light is necessary in bright conditions so a **narrow aperture** (high **f-number**) is used.

f/2.8: wide aperture

In dark conditions a **wide aperture** (low **f-number**) is necessary to let in all available light.

Aperture and depth of field

The **aperture** value also has an effect on the 'depth of field', which describes how much of a photo is in sharp focus.

With a narrow **aperture**, for example f/8.0, more of the photo is in focus.

f/8.0

High f-number: wide depth of field

GADGET TIP! Remember: a higher f-number means more of the photo will be in sharp focus. A lower f-number means less of the photo will be in sharp focus.

With a wide **aperture**, for example f/2.0, less of the photo is in focus.

f/2.0

Low f-number: narrow depth of field

GADGET TIP! Changes in depth of field are most noticeable in photos taken with DSLR cameras (these examples were taken on a DSLR). Depth of field is not as noticeable on point-and-shoot cameras. This is because the lenses on these cameras are not as versatile and are designed to capture a very wide depth of field, whatever the conditions.

Exposure values: **ISO**

The **ISO** value describes the sensitivity of the camera's image sensor to light.

← **Brighter conditions   Darker conditions** →

A **low ISO** indicates a low sensitivity to light and is suited to bright conditions.

A **mid-range ISO** is suited to cloudy or shady conditions.

A **high ISO** indicates a high sensitivity to light and is suited to darker conditions.

INVESTIGATE! What are the highest and lowest ISO values available on your camera?

Some cameras use **ISO** value groupings:

Low: usually ISO 100 or 200.

High: the maximum ISO rating available on your camera.

Auto: the camera sets the ISO automatically.

GADGET TRIVIA! ISO is short for **International Organisation of Standardisation** and refers to the international standard the camera manufacturers use when rating a sensor's sensitivity to light. The International Organisation for Standardisation sets the standard for a wide range of industrial and commercial products, but over time the term **ISO** has become synonymous with a camera sensor's sensitivity rating in photography.

ISO and photo quality

Changing the **ISO** value also changes the photo quality.

Photos taken with a **low ISO** have a very fine-grained appearance.

Photos taken with a **high ISO** can have a grainy appearance. This grain is called **noise** and the amount visible will depend on the make and model of camera.

Remember to select an ISO value appropriate for the lighting conditions.

Using a **low ISO** in bright conditions creates a high quality photo with lots of detail.

However, using a **high ISO** in bright conditions results in a photo with high contrast and less detail.

Using the histogram

Many cameras display a **histogram** on the camera screen. This is a graph which shows the distribution of bright or dark tones in a photo.

The histogram of a balanced exposure has an even distribution, mainly in the centre of the graph.

An underexposed photo has a histogram slanted to the left, as it has captured mostly dark tones.

An overexposed photo has a histogram slanted to the right, as it has captured mostly bright tones.

GADGET TIP! The histogram is a good rough guide as to whether a photo has achieved a balanced exposure, but photos taken in very dark, or very bright conditions always have a natural slant to the left or right.

Exposure value examples

A digital photo is a combination of the three exposure values: shutter speed, aperture and ISO.

Different lighting conditions will use different combinations of exposure values. These examples are a rough guide for three common lighting situations.

Bright conditions

Shutter speed	Fast	1/200 or greater
Aperture	Narrow	f/5.6 or f/8.0
ISO	Low	100 or 200

Cloudy or shady conditions

Shutter speed	Medium	1/160
Aperture	Medium	f/4.0
ISO	Medium	400 or 800

Dark conditions

Shutter speed	Slow	1/80
Aperture	Wide	f/2.8 or less
ISO	High	1600

GADGET TIP! These examples are an approximation to give an idea of how exposure values work in combination. Different exposure values will be needed for different situations.

97

Exposure values quiz

Gadget quiz! Match the photos to the corresponding exposure values.

(answers on the opposite page)

1.

Shutter speed	1/80
Aperture	f/2.8
ISO	1600

2.

Shutter speed	3 seconds
Aperture	f/2.8
ISO	1600

Answer: A-4, B-3, C-1, D-2

3.

Shutter speed	1/500
Aperture	f/4.0
ISO	800

4.

Shutter speed	1/250
Aperture	f/8.0
ISO	100

GADGET TIP! See pages 202-205 for bonus quizzes!

Creative modes

The **creative modes** let the photographer:

- set the exposure values manually and
- change the advanced settings.

Program (P)

 The **ISO** value is set by the user.

Time value (Tv)

 Called **S** on some cameras.

The **shutter speed** is set by the user.

 ISO can also be set, depending on the make and model of camera.

Aperture value (Av)

Called **A** on some cameras.

The **aperture** value is set by the user.

ISO can also be set, depending on the make and model of camera.

Manual

All of the exposure values are set by the user:

- **shutter speed**
- **aperture**
- **ISO**.

Creative mode selection

Creative modes differ between camera makes and models.

Advanced point-and-shoot and DSLR **cameras usually have four creative modes** (for example **P, Tv, Av** and **Manual**).

They can also have **SCENE** modes.

Basic point-and-shoot cameras usually have only one **creative mode** called **P**. In this mode the user can set the **ISO** and the advanced settings. Find out more about **P** mode on page 106.

Some basic point-and-shoot cameras identify their **creative mode** with a camera icon or an **M.** Despite the name **M,** this **creative mode** usually works like **P** mode (see page 106).

Some very simple point-and-shoot cameras don't have any **creative modes**. This can mean:

- advanced settings can only be changed in **AUTO,** or
- there are no advanced settings available on the camera.

INVESTIGATE! Find the creative modes on your camera. Which advanced settings are available in the **creative modes?**

Setting exposure values

Different makes and models of cameras have different solutions for setting exposure values.

On the Gadget Scientist DSLR camera:

- a dial on the top of the camera sets the **shutter speed** ❶
- a dial on the back of the camera sets the **aperture (f-number)** ❷
- the **ISO** is set using a button on the top of the camera. ❸

INVESTIGATE! How do you set the exposure values on your camera?

On the Gadget Scientist point-and-shoot camera the navigation buttons are used to set the exposure values. The up and down buttons set the **shutter speed,** and the left and right buttons set the **aperture.** The **ISO** is set via the **MENU.**

GADGET TIP! Some cameras only use one dial to set the **shutter speed** and **aperture.** In **Tv** mode it sets the **shutter speed,** and in **Av** mode it sets the **aperture.** In **Manual** mode a button changes the dial between setting **shutter speed** or setting **aperture.**

P Creative mode: **P**

In **P** (Program) mode the user sets the **ISO,** and the camera automatically sets the **shutter speed** and **aperture** values.

P mode also allows advanced setting adjustments, for example **exposure compensation** and **white balance.**

Mid-range ISO: shady conditions

INVESTIGATE! Set your camera to **P** mode and display the exposure values on the camera screen. Move between different lighting conditions while changing the **ISO**, and watch how the **shutter speed** and **aperture** values change.

P mode is an ideal way to start using the **creative modes.** It is perfect when moving between different lighting conditions, as the image sensor's sensitivity to light can be changed with one adjustment.

High ISO: low light conditions

GADGET TIP! P mode is like an advanced **AUTO** mode. Although the ISO must be selected, and the flash can be turned on or off, the camera automatically selects the other settings. Also, the advanced settings can be changed.

Tv **S** Creative mode: **Tv** or **S**

In **Tv** or **S** (Time Value or Shutter Speed) mode the user sets the **shutter speed,** and the camera automatically sets the **aperture** and **ISO**.

Tv (or **S**) mode also allows advanced setting adjustments, for example **exposure compensation** and **white balance.**

On many cameras the **ISO** can also be set by the user when in **Tv** mode.

Fast shutter speed: moving subjects

When using **Tv** (or **S**) mode to photograph fast moving subjects in daylight, for example children on slides, on trampolines, or running, select a fast **shutter speed** of 1/250 or above.

When using **Tv** (or **S**) mode in low light conditions select a very slow **shutter speed** and use the camera with a tripod, or rest it on a stable surface.

Slow shutter speed: low light conditions

Creative mode: **Av** or **A**

In **Av** or **A** (Aperture value) mode the user sets the **aperture,** and the camera automatically sets the **shutter speed** and **ISO.**

Av mode also allows advanced setting adjustments, for example **exposure compensation** and **white balance.**

On many cameras the **ISO** can also be set by the user when in **Av** mode.

f/2.0

Low f-number: reduces depth of field

INVESTIGATE! Take two portrait photos: one with a wide aperture (low f-number) and one with narrow aperture (high f-number), and spot the difference!

Adjusting the **aperture** changes the depth of field. For portraits, use a wide **aperture** (low **f-number**). The subject will then be in sharp focus and the background blurry (see opposite page).

For landscapes use a narrow **aperture** (high **f-number**). This increases the depth of field and keeps more of the photo in sharp focus.

f/8.0

High f-number: increases depth of field

GADGET TIP! If you select a narrow aperture, for example f/5.6 or f/8.0, make sure the shutter speed is no slower than 1/80 or your photos could be blurry.

M Creative mode: **Manual**

In **Manual** mode, the user sets all the exposure values: the **shutter speed, aperture** and **ISO.**

One way to use **Manual** mode is to guess the exposure value settings and then take a test shot. If the photo is underexposed or overexposed change the settings and take another photo.

Test photo: underexposed

Manual mode is usually perceived as being for 'experts only', but consider experimenting with **Manual.** The results are immediately visible on the camera screen, and adjustments can be made straight away.

Second photo: balanced exposure

GADGET TIP! Experimenting with **Manual** mode, and making mistakes in the process, is one of the fastest ways to learn how the exposure values work in different lighting conditions.

Advanced settings

The advanced settings are usually available when using a **creative mode** (for example **P, Tv, Av** or **Manual).** These settings give more control over how photos are captured.

Depending on the make and model of camera, the advanced settings are accessed by using the **MENU** or a 'function' (**FUNC** or **Fn**) button and are displayed on the camera screen.

Light meter
(pages 116-119)

Exposure compensation
(pages 120-123)

Exposure lock
(pages 124-125)

White Balance
(pages 126-129)

On the Gadget Scientist camera the advanced settings are shown on the left of the camera screen. They are selected by scrolling through the options on the bottom of the screen. In this example, the **white balance** setting has been set to **Cloudy.**

White balance setting: Cloudy

INVESTIGATE! How do you access and navigate the advanced settings on your camera? (You may have to be in a **creative mode** to try this.)

Advanced settings: **Light meter**

Some cameras have the option to change the **light meter** setting.

The **Evaluative** setting takes multiple readings from the entire photo area to produce an average reading.

The **Centre-weighted** setting takes an average reading from the whole photo area, but prioritises the middle.

The **Spot-reading** takes a reading from the very centre of the photo (about 5% of the photo area).

The **Partial-reading** takes a reading from a slightly larger area than the spot-reading (about 10% of the photo area).

INVESTIGATE! Can you change the **light meter** setting on your camera?

Spot

Partial

Centre

Evaluative

GADGET TIP! Some cameras don't have an option to change the **light meter** setting. On these cameras the **light meter** system is usually **Evaluative.**

117

Light meter examples

 Evaluative setting

The **Evaluative light meter** setting takes an average light reading from an entire photo.

An **Evaluative** reading works best when there are not large variations in the strength of light being captured.

 Evaluative setting

In this example most of the photo is very bright.

By balancing the exposure across the photo the background has been accurately exposed, but the subject is underexposed and very dark.

The **Spot-reading** setting takes a light reading from the centre of a photo.

In this example the subject's face is in the centre of the photo. The background is overexposed, but the subject now has a balanced exposure.

 Spot-reading setting

GADGET TIP! For most photos the **Evaluative light meter** setting works best. Experiment with the **Spot** and **Partial-reading light meter** settings in situations where the photo includes strongly contrasting bright and dark areas.

Advanced settings: **Exposure compensation**

This photo is underexposed because the light meter is adjusting for the subject's bright-coloured t-shirt by letting in less light. The t-shirt is correctly exposed, but most of the photo is underexposed.

In these situations the **exposure compensation** setting can help achieve a balanced exposure.

Some cameras also have a **flash exposure compensation** setting which adjusts the exposure when using flash.

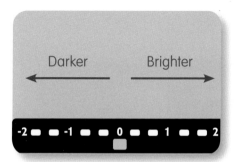

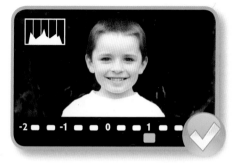

The **exposure compensation** setting changes the exposure of a photo. Moving left along the scale underexposes (darkens) the photo, and moving to the right overexposes (brightens) the photo.

In this example, the original photo (see opposite page) is underexposed. To give the subsequent photo a balanced exposure the **exposure compensation** setting is moved to the right and the photo is taken again.

INVESTIGATE! On some cameras, the **exposure compensation** setting is displayed as numbers between 0 and 2 with + or - next to them. How is the **exposure compensation** setting displayed on your camera?

Using exposure compensation

This photo is overexposed because the light meter is adjusting for the subject's dark-coloured t-shirt by letting in more light. The t-shirt is correctly exposed, but most of the photo is overexposed.

To make subsequent photos darker the **exposure compensation** setting is moved to the left and the photo is taken again.

GADGET TIP! Change the **exposure compensation** setting to zero after you've taken your photos, or the next photos you take may be overexposed or underexposed.

1st photo: underexposed

2nd photo: after adjustment

Use the **exposure compensation** setting **before** a photo is taken if the photo preview on the camera screen looks overexposed or underexposed.

Or, use the **exposure compensation** setting **after** a photo has been taken. If it is overexposed or underexposed then adjust the **exposure compensation** and take the photo again.

GADGET TIP! The exposure compensation setting only adjusts the exposure **before** a photo is taken. To change the exposure of photos already taken, the photo will have to be manipulated on a computer using photo editing software.

Exposure lock

The **exposure lock** feature can be a short-cut to getting a balanced exposure.

Use it when a subject is near a very dark or very bright area, and the camera has set exposure values that have made a photo overexposed or underexposed .

1. Aim the camera at the subject, making sure any very dark or very bright areas near the subject don't appear in the viewfinder, or on the camera screen.

Exposure lock icons

2. Push the exposure lock button, which is usually identified by one of the above icons. The camera will then automatically set the exposure values based on the subject, and not on any of the very dark or very bright areas.

3. Recompose the shot and take the photo. The exposure lock feature only stores the exposure values for 5 to 10 seconds, so don't wait too long!

GADGET TIP! For the best results when using the **exposure lock** feature use the **Spot-reading** or **Partial-reading light meter** setting.

Advanced settings: **White balance**

Human eyes are good at judging what is known as white light. This means a white object always looks white, even in different lighting conditions.

Digital cameras 'see' white light differently. This means photos are sometimes tinged with a colour caused by the type of light used to capture the photo.

INVESTIGATE! Which **white balance** settings are available on your camera?

To take photos without a colour tinge, use the **white balance** setting This adjusts the camera to the type of light available, for example daylight, cloud, or different types of light bulbs.

White balance setting: Tungsten light bulb

The most common **white balance settings** are:

| Average White Balance | Daylight | Cloudy | Tungsten | Fluorescent | Flash |

White balance examples

In this example, a photo taken on a cloudy winter's day has a blue tinge because of the cold, blue winter light.

By using the **Cloudy white balance** setting the photo is warmed up, and skin tones have a more natural colour.

GADGET TIP! Change the **white balance** setting back to **Average** after using the other settings, or your next photos could have odd colour tinges.

Using flash with the **Average white balance (AWB)** setting can result in photos looking cold and blue.

The **Flash white balance** setting warms photos and makes skin tones look natural.

GADGET TIP! White balance settings are a useful feature, but the colour balance of photos can also be changed with photo editing software. This means you can use the **AWB** setting most of the time.

Black and white photos

Low light photos can sometimes look noisy (see page 92).

The noise and imperfections are less noticeable if the photo is changed to black and white.

Photos with an incorrect white balance, for example those taken in tungsten light, can also be improved by changing them to black and white.

GADGET TIP! Black and white photos can look as though they were shot on film and have a retro feel to them.

Some cameras have a setting that allows you to take black and white or sepia photos.

The disadvantage of taking black and white photos is that they will only ever be black and white.

Take all your photos in colour. If you want to make them black and white afterwards, you can ask the photo lab to do this, or change them using photo editing software.

Creative modes summary

1/160, f/5.6, ISO 250

P When in **P** mode remember to change the **ISO** if you move between different lighting conditions.

Use the **exposure compensation** setting if photos are underexposed or overexposed.

1/500, f/4.0, ISO 800

Tv **S** Use for moving subjects when a fast **shutter speed** is necessary, or for night-time photos when a slow **shutter speed** is necessary.

When you are familiar with **Tv** mode, try **Manual** mode.

1/100, f/2.8, ISO 1600

Av **A** Use this mode to experiment with depth of field. A very wide **aperture** (low **f-number**) is ideal for portraits. A narrow **aperture** (high **f-number**) is ideal for landscapes. When you are familiar with **Av** mode, try **Manual** mode.

1/2000, f/2.0, ISO 100

M If you have a DSLR, or an advanced point-and-shoot camera, experiment with taking photos in **Manual** mode.

Remember to set the **ISO, aperture** and **shutter speed** exposure values manually.

Experiment!

These activities are for any make and model of digital camera:

1. Which **creative modes** does your camera have?
2. Which **advanced settings** does your camera have?
3. Take a series of photos without using flash. Use the **exposure compensation** setting to make them brighter or darker.
4. Take a series of **flash** photos. Use the **exposure compensation** setting, or the **flash exposure compensation** setting, to make them lighter or darker.

These activities are for DSLR and advanced point-and-shoot cameras:

1. Identify the buttons and/or dials that allow you to change exposure values.

2. Change to **P** mode and identify the **exposure values** and **advanced settings** on the camera screen.

3. Take photos in bright, shady and dark conditions. Compare the exposure values of your photos with the photos on pages 96-97.

4. Change to **Av** (or **A**) mode and take portraits using a **wide aperture** (low **f-number**), and a **narrow aperture** (high **f-number**). Compare the difference.

5. Change to **Tv** (or **S**) mode. Use a tripod to take a photo in dark conditions with a slow **shutter speed**, for example, 1 second or more.

6. Change to **Manual** mode. Use the exposure values on pages 96-97 as a guide to take photos in bright, shady and dark conditions. Change the exposure values until you get a balanced exposure.

How do I improve composition?

One way to improve composition, especially landscapes, is to use the **rule of thirds.** Put the subject about a third of the way from the edge of the photo, and either to the side, or above or below the horizon.

The **rule of thirds** also works when taking portraits. Compositions can be made more interesting by placing the subject to the left or right of the photo.

How do I choose a background?

Avoid distracting backgrounds, or objects coming out of people's heads. For example, plants, trees, lamp-posts or road signs.

Look for backgrounds which don't distract from the subject. Sometimes moving a metre or two (5 or 6 feet) left or right can make all the difference.

This doesn't mean backgrounds have to be boring. This bright-blue background is actually a garage door!

Sometimes unusual backgrounds can add interest to a portrait.

GADGET TIP! When taking portraits with backgrounds like the graffiti photo above, also take an alternative with a neutral background. You'll then have two very different photos to choose from!

How do I identify flattering light?

Hard light

The direct sunlight in this photo has created high-contrast shadows on the subject's face. High-contrast or **hard** light, with strong shadows, is ideal for portraits of rugged actors, but not necessarily family photos!

Soft light

This photo was taken in the same room, but away from direct sunlight. There are no hard shadows, and the low-contrast or **soft** light flatters the subject.

Flash

The light from camera flash is a **hard** light. It can be unflattering and emphasise and exaggerate blemishes and wrinkles.

No flash

Photos taken using natural light during the daytime, or artificial light in darker conditions, tend to be more flattering.

GADGET TIP! Sometimes simply moving a subject a metre or two (5 or 6 feet) to the left or right can transform the lighting effects in a photo.

How do I use flattering light?

Using soft light for portraits suits all age groups, but it's particularly flattering for the senior generation. Soft light doesn't accentuate wrinkles and can make people look younger than they are.

One of the best times to take photos is late in the day. The light is soft and usually has a warm glow.

INVESTIGATE! The first and last hours of sunlight are called the **golden hour** by photographers. Capture this soft light by taking a landscape photo as the sun rises and a portrait photo as the sun sets.

How do I photograph landscapes?

Use the **Landscape SCENE.** This automatically sets a narrow **aperture** (high **f-number**) and increases the depth of field, which keeps more of the photo in focus.

Or, use the **Av** (or **A**) or **Manual** mode and set a narrow **aperture** (high **f-number**), for example f/5.6 or f/8.0.

INVESTIGATE! Next time you photograph a landscape try framing the scene with trees or flowers. In the above example the foliage in the foreground frames the photo and makes an interesting composition.

Include more of the sky when it's doing something interesting. In this photo, the cloud formations are the primary feature of the landscape.

Landscape photos don't have to include the sky. If the sky isn't interesting don't include it!

GADGET TIP! In landscapes that include water, look for reflections. These can add interest and may even become the primary feature of your photo.

How do I get creative with landscapes?

When photographing landscapes take a horizontal and a vertical photo. Sometimes, just changing orientation like this can create a more interesting composition.

GADGET TIP! Notice how hard light has been used in these landscape photos. Unlike portraits, contrasting light in landscapes can create depth and interest.

Landscape photos don't have to be of a view! Sometimes there are fascinating photos to be found at ground level. For example, the rocks and stream in the photo above.

Streams, ponds and the beach all provide great opportunities for small-scale landscapes, and it's also a chance to use the **macro** setting (see page 58).

GADGET TIP! When taking a landscape photo, look down to see if there is an interesting scene near your feet as well!

How do I help people relax?

Some people hate being photographed as they feel uncomfortable being the centre of attention. If they've had bad photos taken in the past they can be reluctant to repeat the experience!

To help persuade unwilling subjects suggest going somewhere without an audience. Help your subjects relax by giving them a big smile before taking their photo.

When photographing adults ask them to smile and look straight into the lens.

When photographing children be imaginative. Tell them there's a small dinosaur in the camera and ask them to watch carefully to see if it has red or green eyes when the photo is being taken.

GADGET TIP! Politely discourage other people trying to attract your subject's attention as they may look in a different direction or feel uncomfortable.

How do I photograph portraits?

Use the **Portrait SCENE**. This automatically sets a wide **aperture** (low **f-number**) and creates a narrow depth of field.

Av **M** Or, use the **Av** (or **A**) or **Manual** mode and set a wide **aperture**, for example f/3.5 or f/2.8.

Q Photograph portraits from about 2 metres (6 feet) away. Use **zoom** to help frame a head-shot, even if you're near your subject.

 People can blink when being photographed, so use the **continuous** setting to help capture them with their eyes open at least once!

During the daytime, turn the flash off and use natural light as it's more flattering!

GADGET TIP! Take a series of photos: vertical, horizontal and with alternative backgrounds. This gives you and your subject different types of photos to choose from.

How do I photograph children?

In this photo the photographer is standing over the child with other adults watching. This is making the child feel uncomfortable and unhappy. The hard flash light is also unflattering.

GADGET TIP! Don't make a photo a battle of wills with a child. At a different time or day they may be more receptive, but if they've been forced to be in a photo they may refuse to co-operate the next time around.

In this photo a completely different approach has been taken. There's no audience around and the photographer is kneeling down and at eye level to the child. The child is relaxed and happy, and the soft natural light is flattering.

GADGET TIP! Take a photo with a favourite toy or something special to the child. Then it is 'their' photo and not yours.

How do I photograph families?

This family photo has a distracting background, one of the children is upset, and the adults look awkward and uncomfortable trying to hold the children.

In this photo the subjects look content. They are seated and relaxed and the photographer has chosen a time when the children are happy. In other words, when they are not tired or hungry!

GADGET TIP! When photographing a family or group try and arrange subjects so their faces are close together, but not in front of each other.

How do I arrange groups and families?

Very often people lean or put their arm around the person next to them when they are being photographed. This can make them look awkward and uncomfortable and results in an unflattering photo.

GADGET TIP! Before taking a portrait, stop, lower the camera, and look at the people being photographed. Ask yourself, is it a good background? Is the light flattering? Do they look comfortable? Is there anything I should change?

Before taking a photo help your subjects to arrange themselves comfortably, and make them feel relaxed. And remember, no leaning!

GADGET TIP! Usually there's no rush to take a photo so ignore the impulse to take it quickly. Most people appreciate any extra time taken to organise a flattering photo, as they'll look better as a result.

How do I photograph groups?

Group photos don't just arrange themselves. If the photographer doesn't get involved then people can be hidden and won't look comfortable.

Don't be afraid to take a couple of minutes to arrange a group photo. People are usually grateful to be told where to sit and stand! Chairs, or a bench in this example, help make sure no-one is hiding.

In family photos adults can be distracted by what their young children are looking at or doing.

Ask the adults and older children to smile and look at the camera. Concentrate on getting the adults attention first. A baby looking elsewhere or waving their arms won't spoil a photo, but an adult doing the same thing will!

GADGET TIP! A funny noise, or a soft toy put on the photographer's head can help attract a younger child's attention!

How do I photograph pets?

When taking photos of pets use the same techniques as when photographing children:

- don't use flash
- don't stand over them
- don't try and take a photo if there is an audience.

Instead, find a quiet moment and:

• use natural light, and
• photograph them at eye level, perhaps by putting them on a sofa or couch.

How do I take holiday photos?

If you look hard enough you can see the subject of this photo standing outside Buckingham Palace. This is a classic holiday snap with the subject lost in the scene.

In this photo the subject is near the photographer. The photographer is concentrating on the subject looking happy, while letting the landmark add extra interest without dominating the photo.

GADGET TIP! Think of holiday photos as portraits with interesting backgrounds, rather than trying to squeeze every detail into the scene.

How do I take candid photos?

Many people like the natural and relaxed look of candid photos where the subject doesn't know they're being photographed.

  Use the **Kids & Pets** or **Sports SCENE**. This automatically sets a fast **shutter speed** which helps freeze fleeting expressions.

Tv **M** Or, use the **Tv** (or **S**) or **Manual** mode and set a fast **shutter speed** of 1/200 or above.

Q Use **zoom** to help keep a discreet distance. A good technique is to photograph at an angle, or over the shoulder of the person the subject is talking to.

Candid shots need patience: wait for your subject to smile, and try not to take unflattering shots when they are eating or drinking.

How do I take action photos?

  Use the **Kids & Pets** or **Sports SCENE**. This automatically sets a fast **shutter** speed which helps freeze moving subjects.

 Or, use the **Tv** (or **S**) or **Manual** mode and set a fast **shutter speed** of 1/250 or above.

 GADGET TIP! Get as close to your subjects as possible before taking photos, as this helps create the impression that you're part of the action.

 Look for moments where subjects are interacting and take a burst of photos using the **continuous** setting. This gives you a wider range of photos to choose from.

GADGET TIP! Look for an 'action-reaction' moment when one subject responds to what another subject is doing.

How do I photograph people in bright sunlight?

Sunshine creates hard shadows on people's faces and can make them squint.

Photograph portraits in the shade. This eliminates hard shadows, squinting eyes and it also means the subject feels more comfortable.

⚡ If there's no shade available use flash to reduce shadows on faces. This technique is called **fill-in-flash** because it 'fills-in' the shadows.

P Use **P** mode and set a low **ISO**, for example ISO 100 or ISO 200.

 Or, use the **Beach** or **Snow SCENE** which automatically sets a low **ISO.**

How do I use daylight indoors?

Try not to take photos with the camera pointing towards the primary light source.

In this example the light source is behind the subject, which results in the subject being 'back-lit'.

This makes it hard for the camera to focus, and without using the light meter or exposure compensation settings the subject will be underexposed.

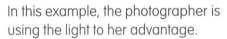

In this example, the photographer is using the light to her advantage.

The light source is now behind the photographer and illuminates the

subject's face. This results in a fast-to-focus, accurately exposed and much more flattering photo.

GADGET TIP! Use windows or doorways to achieve this flattering lighting. Avoid locations where there's too much bright sunlight streaming in, but if there's daylight outside, then you shouldn't have to use flash inside!

How do I take flash photos?

 Use **P** mode which automatically sets **shutter speed** and **aperture.**

Turn the **flash** on.

Select an **ISO** of 200.

If the photo is overexposed or underexposed use the **flash exposure compensation** setting and take the photo again (see pages 120-123).

Try not to take flash photos with glass or mirrors in the background as these create distracting reflections of the flash light.

M Experiment with **flash** in **Manual** mode with the exposure values:

- 1/125
- f/5.6
- ISO 200.

Use the **flash exposure compensation** setting if necessary.

How do I photograph sunsets and nightscapes?

Flash photos of sunsets and night landscapes illuminate the foreground, but not the background. Also, these types of flash photos don't capture any mood or atmosphere.

Tv Use **Tv** (or **S**) mode and:

- turn the **flash** off and use a tripod
- select the highest **ISO**
- select a **shutter speed** of 1/30.

Take a test shot and if necessary change the **shutter speed.**

M Experiment in **Manual** mode with the exposure values:

- 1/30
- f/2.8
- ISO 1600, and use a tripod.

Take a test shot and if necessary change the exposure values.

GADGET TIP! If your camera doesn't have **creative modes** use **AUTO,** a tripod and turn the **flash** off.

How do I take photos at night?

Standard flash settings
1/125, f/5.6, ISO 200

P **⚡** A standard flash photo illuminates subjects who are near the photographer, but far-off backgrounds stay dark.

Night SCENE settings
1/10, f/4.0, ISO 800

The **Night SCENE** automatically sets a high ISO, slow shutter speed and flash. This illuminates both the subject and the background. Use a tripod or a stable surface to prevent blur.

**Night SCENE settings
1/10, f/4.0, ISO 800**

The **Night SCENE** works best when using a tripod, as the slow shutter speed can cause blurry photos.

**Night Snapshot SCENE settings
1/20, f/5.6 ISO 1600**

The **Night Snapshot SCENE** automatically sets a slow shutter speed, but not as slow as the **Night SCENE**. The flash freezes subjects in the foreground, while the background is blurry. Ideal for parties.

INVESTIGATE! Experiment with taking photos at night in **Manual** mode. Begin by using the exposure values from the photo captions above.

How do I photograph fireworks?

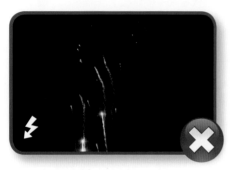

This photo of fireworks was taken using flash.

This has frozen the fireworks in mid-flight and not captured any movement.

This photo used the **Fireworks SCENE** which automatically selects a very slow **shutter speed** of 1 second or more.

However, because the camera was not used with a tripod this photo is blurry.

This photo used the **Fireworks SCENE** with a tripod. The slow **shutter speed** captured the light from the fireworks streaking across the sky and the tripod means the photo is not blurry.

INVESTIGATE! Experiment with taking photos of fireworks in **Manual** mode, without using flash. Suggested exposure values are: **2 seconds, f/2.8** and **ISO 1600.**

How do I take low light photos with a DSLR?

1/60: camera shake

Hand-held photos taken using a **shutter speed** below 1/80 are usually blurry.

1/80: no camera shake

M Use **Manual** mode and:

- turn the **flash** off
- select the highest **ISO**
- select the widest **aperture** (lowest **f-number**)
- set the **shutter speed** to 1/80.

If the photo is overexposed:
- increase the **shutter speed**
- and/or increase the **f-number.**

If the photo is underexposed:
- set the **shutter speed** below 1/80 and
- use a tripod, or rest the camera on a stable surface.

GADGET TIP! Hand-held photos using **shutter speeds** less than 1/80 are possible on some cameras if they are held very steady (see next page). Find the slowest **shutter speed** possible on your camera by taking a series of test shots.

How do I improve low light photos?

Reduce camera shake in low light by holding the camera with both hands. To make yourself steady push the camera against your eyebrow.

INVESTIGATE! Some cameras have an especially light-sensitive ISO 3200. What's the highest ISO available on your camera?

Use the **wide-angle** setting to take low light photos and don't use telephoto (zoom in). The telephoto setting reduces the light that is let into the camera.

Use a tripod, or improvise one by using a stack of books. Make sure they are stable and there is no risk of your camera falling on the ground.

 GADGET TIP! Take low light photos in the brightest places in dark rooms, for example near to lamps or other light sources.

Experiment!

Now try out everything you've learnt by shooting a photo project.

Start by photographing your life!

Imagine you need a set of photos to show a friend from another country. Take photos of your home, your neighbourhood, your favourite things and your friends and family.

Think of your photo project as telling a story. You could even photograph it as 'A day in your life'.

1. Photograph your home. Take photos from different angles and experiment with composition.

2. Take landscape photos of your street, your garden, or parks close to your home. Include some detail shots using macro.

3. Take a group photo of your family or friends. Arrange the photo so there are no distractions and people aren't leaning awkwardly.

4. Take a series of portraits using the techniques suggested in this guide. Remember to use locations with suitable backgrounds and with soft, flattering light. Take the portraits:

   • inside using window light
   • outside in the shade
   • in low light conditions without flash.

5. Take a series of action photos. This could be friends or family (or pets!) playing sport, or candid shots of people chatting and interacting together.

Batteries

The battery life display on digital cameras can be misleading. For example, a battery display can show 'full' for some time and then change to 'empty' very quickly.

Full

Partial Power

Almost empty

Empty

GADGET TIP! Buy a spare battery so you can still take photos even if the first battery runs out. Also, before going anywhere with your camera, remember to recharge your batteries!

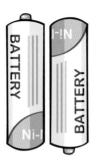

Rechargeable batteries maintain a constant output before running out of power quickly. Standard batteries, however, gradually run out of power. This is particularly noticeable when using flash, as standard batteries take longer and longer to recycle the flash.

A digital camera uses only one type of battery so check the battery type before buying a spare.

GADGET TIP! Take your battery charger and a power converter when going on holiday.

Memory cards

There are four main memory card formats available for digital cameras: Secure Digital™ (SD), CompactFlash™, xD Picture Card™ and Memory Stick™.

The storage capacity of memory cards is measured in megabytes (MB) and gigabytes (GB). Common card sizes are 1GB, 2GB and 4GB. The larger the memory card capacity, the more photos and videos it can store.

The memory card is usually found near the batteries, or has a separate slot (depending on the make and model of camera).

Memory cards are usually removed from the camera by gently pulling them out, or sometimes they have to be pushed in slightly before they 'pop' out.

GADGET TIP! When buying new memory cards buy the format made to fit your camera! Buy a large capacity memory card, for example 2GB or 4GB, so you can store more photos on it.

Downloading memory cards

When a memory card is full, download it to a computer.

The photos from the card can then be organised and edited using:

- software that came with the camera
- free photo editing software or
- professional photo editing software.

Photos can then be:

- copied to a CD or DVD and taken to a photo lab for printing
- uploaded to an online photo printing service
- printed at home
- shared online
- backed up!

Memory cards can also be taken to a photo lab and photos printed directly, or copied to a CD or DVD.

GADGET TIP! Ask for an extra copy of the CD or DVD containing your photos. Then you have a backup if there is a problem with the original CD or DVD.

Protecting memory cards

Memory cards are intended as temporary storage devices. If a card fails, all the photos and videos stored on it will be lost.

Keep memory cards protected:

- use a memory card case when they're not in the camera
- don't leave them in direct sunlight
- keep them away from water, sand and magnets.

Format

Format card

Cancel | OK

Memory cards should only be formatted after the photos on them have been downloaded and backed up.

Formatting recreates the file structure that organises and stores the photos on a memory card. This prevents conflicts in the file structure that can make a card fail.

Format memory cards 'in-camera' rather than on a computer. The option to format a memory card in-camera can usually be selected in the MENU.

Format new memory cards before using them for the first time, or when using an old memory card in a new camera.

GADGET TIP! When a memory card is formatted all photos on it are erased - **permanently**. Only format a card after all the photos on it are downloaded and backed up.

Megapixels and file size

Digital cameras capture photos on a sensor. The size of the sensor is rated in megapixels.

The Gadget Scientist point-and-shoot is a 12 megapixel camera.

Cameras with more megapixels capture larger file sizes. A larger file size results in a photo with more detail, or higher image resolution.

The Gadget Scientist DSLR is a 15 megapixel camera because it has a larger sensor.

This sensor has a higher overall performance compared to the point-and-shoot. For example it captures a larger file size, as well as a larger range of colour and contrast.

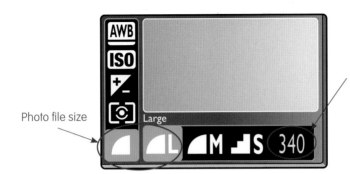

Photo file size

Number of photos that can be stored on the memory card using the selected file size

Whichever type of camera you are using, point-and-shoot or DSLR, select the largest file size available. This uses the full megapixel capability of the camera and achieves the highest quality photo resolution.

Photo file size can usually be changed in the MENU. Some cameras specify numerical photo sizes, for example 4000x3000 pixels, others use categories, for example Large, Medium and Small.

INVESTIGATE! How many megapixels is your camera?

Why file size matters

The smallest file size setting on a camera captures photos with limited detail, or **low resolution** images.

Low resolution images have a fuzzy appearance when viewed on a computer or television screen, or printed on photographic paper.

Small file size setting

By using the largest file size setting this photo has captured the maximum level of detail available and is a **high resolution** image.

High resolution images are clear and crisp when viewed on a computer or television screen, or printed on photographic paper.

Large file size setting

GADGET TIP! A small file size setting means more photos can be stored on a memory card, but will be low resolution images. If you have to store more photos use a larger memory card.

Photo file formats

JPEG Digital cameras use two different file formats for storing images: JPEG or 'raw'.

JPEG is the only option on most point-and-shoot cameras.

JPEG is a standard file format and can be viewed on most computers without requiring specialised software.

RAW A raw file format is usually available on DSLR cameras and is the common choice of professional and advanced amateur photographers.

Raw files record a wider range of colour and contrast compared to JPEG files. They are larger sized files and therefore use more space on a memory card.

Raw files need specialised software for viewing and editing

INVESTIGATE! Which file formats does your camera support?

Backing up photos

If a computer fails all the data stored on it can be lost.

If your computer fails you could lose years of family photos and memories.

Back up your photos!

It's a boring task, but if your computer fails you'll be very glad you did it.

Suggested backup process

1. Download photos from memory cards to a computer regularly, and save them in folders based on events or subjects. For example, 'Family Holiday' or 'Spring Wildflowers'.

This backup protects against memory card failure.

2. When the photos have been downloaded to a computer, copy them to an external hard drive.

This backup protects against computer failure.

3. Burn a CD or DVD of the downloaded photos. Label it with the date and folder description, and keep it at a friend's or family member's house.

This backup protects against flood, fire or any other disaster at home.

GADGET TIP! By investing in an external hard drive you can back up everything on your computer - not just photos!

Bonus exposure values quiz 1

Gadget quiz! Match the photos to the corresponding exposure values. (answers on the opposite page)

1.
Shutter speed	1/200
Aperture	f/8.0
ISO	100

2.
Shutter speed	1/100
Aperture	f/2.8
ISO	1600

3.

Shutter speed	1/500
Aperture	f/4.0
ISO	400

4.

Shutter speed	1/15
Aperture	f/5.6
ISO	1600

Bonus exposure values quiz 2

Gadget quiz! Match the photos to the corresponding exposure values
(answers on the opposite page)

1.

Shutter speed	1/80
Aperture	f/2.0
ISO	1600

2.

Shutter speed	1/160
Aperture	f/4.0
ISO	800

3.

Shutter speed	1/800
Aperture	f/2.0
ISO	100

4.

Shutter speed	1/125
Aperture	f/8.0
ISO	100

The Gadget Scientist supports...

The Gadget Scientist supports **Mibila Village Clinic.**

This project provides primary healthcare and clean water to approximately 5,000 people in rural Zambia.

This support is made via **Dignity (Worldwide),** registered charity number 1122656.

The clinic provides pre- and postnatal care, immunisations, mosquito nets to help prevent malaria, education programmes and a wide range of other medical services.

Mibila Village Clinic: the word **Handenu** means **be healed**

To find out more about Mibila Village Clinic visit the Gadget Scientist website.
www.gadgetscientist.com

Index

The Gadget Scientist Guide to Using Your Digital Camera

Mark Burton